the Write Words the Write Words the Write
Write Words the Write Words the Write
the Write Words the Write Words th
Write Words the Write Words the Write
the Write Words the Write Words th
Write Words the Write Words the Write
the Write Words the Write Words th
Write Words the Write Words the Write
the Write Words the Write Words th
Write Words the Write Words the Write
the Write Words the Write Words th
Write Words the Write Words the Write
the Write Words the Write Words th
Write Words the Write Words the Write

the Write Words

ART AS WORDS • WORDS AS ART

Kathy Davis

simple truths ®
Your Destination For Inspiration
an imprint of Sourcebooks, Inc.

Published by Simple Truths, an imprint of Sourcebooks, Inc.
P.O. Box 4410, Naperville, Illinois 60567-4410
(630) 961-3900
Fax: (630) 961-2168
www.sourcebooks.com

Printed and bound in the United States of America.
WOZ 10 9 8 7 6 5 4 3 2 1

This book is dedicated
to all the dreamers and realists
throughout history who have found just
the right words to express themselves.
Because their ideas are often timeless,
finding a home deep in our hearts and
minds, we relate to their words as if
they're our own.
We know we could never have found the
right words to have said it better.
Over time, these quotations become
our talismans, our touchstones,
our peace of mind.

Thanks to all those eloquent writers
and philosophers whose words
appear in these pages.
Every attempt has been made to give
proper attribution
to the authors.

Kathy Davis

A

NOTE

FROM

THE

AUTHOR

THE WRITE WORDS

I HAVE ALWAYS BEEN TAKEN WITH THE POWER OF WORDS, AND I'VE ALWAYS WANTED TO CREATE A BOOK WHERE WORDS TOOK CENTER STAGE—IN THE SPIRIT OF GRAFFITI-AS-ART.

MY BACKGROUND IN CALLIGRAPHY INTRODUCED ME TO MANY DIFFERENT TYPES OF LETTERING TOOLS. I CHOSE A POINTED BRUSH TO HELP COMMUNICATE THE EMOTION IN THE MEANING OF THE WORDS IN THIS BOOK. THE MIX OF WATERCOLOR AND BOLD GRAPHICS LENDS SOME VARIETY TO THE PAGE LAYOUTS. IN THESE PAGES YOU'LL FIND SIMPLE SAYINGS THAT MAY INSPIRE, PROVOKE THOUGHT, COMMUNICATE AN EMOTION, OR PRODUCE A SMILE, ALL PRESENTED IN A STRAIGHTFORWARD, UNCOMPLICATED FORMAT.

I HOPE YOU FIND MANY SAYINGS IN THIS BOOK THAT SPEAK TO YOU, AND I HOPE YOU AGREE THAT *THE WRITE WORDS* TELLS IT LIKE IT IS!

Kathy Davis

Make your life a work of ART

You know
all
those things
you've always
wanted to do?

You should go DO THEM.

Lara Casey

New Beginnings

come at every stage of life

The best is yet to be.
—Robert Browning

think positively
eat healthy work
harder dance
worry less
Be

exercise daily

hard play

often build faith

Read more

HAPPY

the Sky's the Limit

when
your
Heart's
in it.

I AM AN OLD MAN AND HAVE KNOWN
A GREAT MANY TROUBLES, BUT
MOST OF THEM NEVER HAPPENED.
—MARK TWAIN

Worrying
is like
praying
for what
you
don't
want.

Get out of your own way.

Steve Maraboli

ONCE YOU MAKE A DECISION,
THE UNIVERSE CONSPIRES
TO MAKE IT HAPPEN.
—RALPH WALDO EMERSON

You have to
leave
the city
of
your comfort
and
go into
the wilderness
of
your intuition.

What you'll
discover
will be
wonderful.

What you'll
discover
is
yourself.
—Alan Alda

REMEMBER

THE MOMENTS

OF THE

PAST,

LOOK FORWARD

TO THE

PROMISE

OF THE

FUTURE,

BUT MOST OF ALL,

CELEBRATE

THE PRESENT,

FOR IT IS

PRECIOUS.

Stay
close
to
anything that
makes you
glad
you are
alive

Hafez

gine

THE FUTURE BELONGS TO THOSE WHO BELIEVE IN THE BEAUTY OF THEIR DREAMS.
— ELEANOR ROOSEVELT

BELIEVE WITH ALL OF YOUR HEART THAT YOU WILL DO WHAT YOU WERE MADE TO DO.
— ORISON SWETT MARDEN

HAPPY ARE THOSE WHO DREAM DREAMS AND ARE READY TO PAY THE PRICE TO MAKE THEM COME TRUE.
— LEON J. SUENES

DREAM NO SMALL DREAMS FOR THEY HAVE NO POWER TO MOVE THE HEARTS OF MEN.
— JOHANN WOLFGANG VON GOETHE

TO ACCOMPLISH GREAT THINGS, WE MUST NOT ONLY ACT, BUT ALSO DREAM; NOT ONLY PLAN, BUT ALSO BELIEVE.
— ANATOLE FRANCE

A DREAM DOESN'T BECOME REALITY THROUGH MAGIC; IT TAKES SWEAT, DETERMINATION, AND HARD WORK.
— COLIN POWELL

it's

ok

to color
outside the
lines.

be
truthful,
gentle,
and

fear

less

Gandhi

THE GREATEST MISTAKE
YOU CAN MAKE IN LIFE
IS TO BE CONTINUALLY FEARING
YOU WILL MAKE ONE.
—ELBERT HUBBARD

choose to Shine.

time to
drink
Champagne
&
dance
on
the
table!

IF YOU OBEY ALL THE RULES,
YOU MISS ALL THE FUN.

—KATHARINE HEPBURN

i'm going to look for the good in today.

O ME, EVERY HOUR OF THE DAY AND NIGHT IS AN UNSPEAKABLY PERFECT MIRACLE.—WALT WHITMAN

DON'T PUT OFF YOUR HAPPY LIFE.

Create
a life
you
Love

WHEN LIFE HANDS
YOU LEMONS,
MAKE
A
VODKA AND TONIC.

MY BRAIN has too many Tabs open.

When
Nothing
goes
Right.

Go
Left.

You never know how strong you are ...

until
being strong
is the only choice
you have.

Author Unknown

You can't
Rush Something
You want
to last

forever

Author Unknown

Do MORE of What BRings you JOY

Stop. Lo

ok. listen.

BE COLORFUL.
BE BRAVE.
BE BRILLIANT.
BE TRUE TO WHO YOU ARE.
BE THANKFUL.
BE STILL.
BE FIERCE.
BE EXCEPTIONAL.

be.
here.
Now.

let your feet
follow your he

art...

Celtic Saying

just keep going

MANY OF LIFE'S
FAILURES ARE
PEOPLE WHO DID NOT
REALIZE HOW CLOSE
THEY WERE TO
SUCCESS WHEN
THEY GAVE UP.
—THOMAS EDISON

IT DOES NOT
MATTER HOW SLOWLY
YOU GO AS LONG AS
YOU DO NOT STOP.
—CONFUCIUS

RIVERS KNOW THIS:
THERE IS NO HURRY.
WE SHALL GET THERE
SOME DAY.
—A. A. MILNE,
WINNIE-THE-POOH

spread kindness

scatter
joy

LAUGHTER IS THE
SHORTEST DISTANCE
BETWEEN TWO PEOPLE.
—VICTOR BORGE

i love
the people who
can make
me
laugh
when i feel
like i can't
even
smile

EVERYONE SHOULD
CAREFULLY OBSERVE
WHICH WAY HIS
HEART DRAWS HIM,
AND THEN CHOOSE
THAT WAY WITH ALL
HIS STRENGTH.

—HASIDIC SAYING

Place your Heart above your mind.

do
small things
with
great
LOVE

Mother Teresa

WHEREVER THERE IS
A HUMAN BEING,
THERE IS
AN OPPORTUNITY
FOR A KINDNESS.
—LUCIUS ANNAEUS SENECA

ALL THINGS GROW
WITH LOVE.
—PROVERB

HOW BEAUTIFUL
A DAY CAN BE WHEN
KINDNESS TOUCHES IT!
—GEORGE ELLISTON

ONCE WE ACCEPT
OUR LIMITS,
WE GO BEYOND
THEM.
—ALBERT EINSTEIN

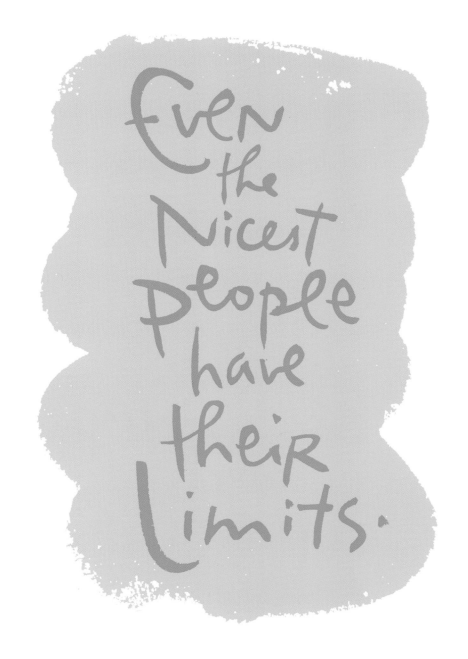

Even the Nicest People have their Limits.

Sometimes you just have to take a Nap and get over it.

Maura Stuard

EXPECT TROUBLE AS AN INEVITABLE PART OF LIFE AND
REPEAT TO YOURSELF, THE MOST COMFORTING WORDS OF
ALL: THIS, TOO, SHALL PASS.

— ANN LANDERS

Never again.

until
next
time.

New

Every
once in a while
everyone needs
a good

Stay Under
the
Covers Day.

For fast-acting relief,
try slowing down.

—Lily Tomlin

be
a
Voice

not

an

Echo

Albert Einstein

Raise your words Not your voice.

it is RAIN that grows

flowers, Not thunder.

Rumi

keep
your words
soft and
sweet...

in case
you have
to
eat
them.

Andy Rooney

Be happy,
it drives
People
CRaZY.

good
people
bring out
the
good
in
people

As we express our gratitude,
we must never forget that
the highest appreciation
is not to utter words,
but to live by them.
— John F. Kennedy

There is a calmness to a
life lived in gratitude,
a quiet joy.
— Ralph H. Blum

There are only two ways to live your life.
One is as though nothing is a miracle.
The other is as though everything is a miracle.
— Albert Einstein

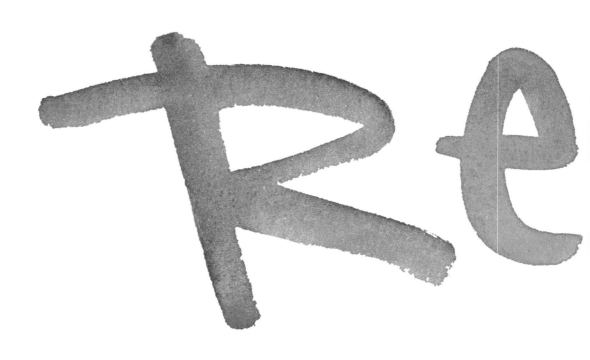

Be filled
with
WONDER

Be
touched
by
Peace

ABOUT THE AUTHOR

Embracing her lifelong dream for a career with creative freedom, Kathy Davis launched her company in 1990. Today, the former teacher turned artist and entrepreneur guides a growing staff and an extensive portfolio of nearly 40,000 images, acting as chief visionary of the company that bears her name. She is now one of America's leading social expression designers.

Kathy's colorful art and inspiring messages are now being seen on lifestyle products she creates in the gift, home decor, fashion, and social expression industries, and her brand touches more than 70 million consumers worldwide each year. She is also the author of multiple books, including: *Scatter Joy—Create a Life You Love*, *Simple Secrets: 7 Principles to Inspire Success*, and *Love Blooms in a Mother's Heart: A Celebration of Motherhood*.

Kathy's brand promise to "Scatter Joy: Joy through Art, Joy through Living, Joy through Giving" permeates all of her designs. Her brand promise is also expressed through her company's charitable giving efforts and support of the arts. Ultimately, her dream is to create a Scatter Joy Center for the Arts.

Kathy's work reflects her lifestyle and the things that inspire her life as a mother, wife, and career woman. Her love of nature, understanding of people, and desire to give back to the world are driving forces in her creative process.

For more information, visit www.kathydavis.com.

Need a Boost?

Visit **www.simpletruths.com** to explore
our entire collection of gift books—
perfect for friends, family, or employees.

Visit **www.simpletruthsmovies.com** to access our
FREE library of inspirational videos!

Or call us toll-free at **1-800-900-3427**